# Courage, Sacrifice, and Honor: Tales from the Frontline Heroes

Jim Stephens

Published by RWG Publishing, 2023.

While every precaution has been taken in the preparation of this book, the publisher assumes no responsibility for errors or omissions, or for damages resulting from the use of the information contained herein.

COURAGE, SACRIFICE, AND HONOR: TALES FROM THE FRONTLINE HEROES

**First edition. May 7, 2023.**

Copyright © 2023 Jim Stephens.

Written by Jim Stephens.

# Also by Jim Stephens

Kindle Publishing Made Easy: Autopilot Cash With Amazon Kindle!
Million-Dollar Secrets of the Amazon Associates: How They Make Money From the Biggest Online Shopping Mall
Self-Publishing Made Easy: The Easy Way to Self-publish Your Own Books!
Scam Busters: How to Avoid the Most Popular Scams of Today!
Affiliate Marketing and Blogging
The Quick and Easy Guide of Diamonds
Government Information
Hiking and Camping
Koi Pond
Law Information Guide
Motor Homes Research
Affiliate Marketing and Success Systems
Online Shopping
Outsourcing Ebooks and Software Jobs
Personal Loans
Private Jet Charters
Private Yacht Charters
Internet Marketer Alpha Dog
Networking and Social Dominance in the Twenty-First Century
Copywriting Best Kept Secrets: A Training Course for Writing Great Copy
Starting Your Home Business

Affiliate Marketing for Beginners: You Will Never Succeed Unless You Take The Opportunity

A Guide to Creating the Most Appropriate Budgets for You: Additional Cash in Your Pocket

Various Advantages of Membership Websites: With Membership Websites, Create a Passive Income

Affiliate Marketing Made Simple: Avoid Common Errors and Thrive in Successes

Article Marketing Made Simple: It Is Not Necessarily Difficult to Succeed

Blogging Made Simple: Blogging Can Be Lucrative

Advertising That Pays: Increase Your Traffic and Leads

The Complete Guide to Copywriting: Creating Words That Sell

Affiliate Marketing Made Simple

The Affiliate Marketer's Manual

Aquarium Maintenance Made Simple

Beginner's Guide to Online Video Marketing

Blogging Fundamentals: Blogging is the Next Big Thing

Techniques for Advanced Search Engine Optimization: On Autopilot, Increase Your Traffic and Profits!

Article Marketing Secrets

Beginner's Guide to Black Hat SEO

Super Guide to Snowmobiling: The Best Places to Have a Great Time

Forest Adventure With Friends: A Captivating Story With a Lot of Fun

How to Advertise Like a Pro

My Journey Through Life: A Personal Memoir

The Art of Crafting Short Stories: A Guide to Writing and Publishing

The Ultimate Guide to Making Money Online: Proven Strategies and Tips for Success

Battlefield of Honor: Bravery and Sacrifice Tested In Ultimate Battle

Echoes of the Past: Unveiling History's Secrets

Warrior's Code: The Unbreakable Ethics of a Warrior

AI-Powered Marketing: The Future of Digital Advertising

Beyond Words: How ChatGPT is Revolutionizing Communication
The Language of AI: Exploring the Power of ChatGPT
Talking to Machines: The Fascinating Story of ChatGPT and AI Language Models
Uncovering the Unknown: Tales of Mysterious Discoveries
Shadow Squadron: Inside Covert Operations
The Last Stand: The Triumph of Bravery in Desperate Times
Valor in the Skies: Courage and Sacrifice in Aerial Warfare
Courage, Sacrifice, and Honor: Tales from the Frontline Heroes

# Table of Contents

Chapter 1: The Call to Duty: Why They Served ............ 1
Chapter 2: In the Trenches: Surviving the Frontline ............ 3
Chapter 3: A Band of Brothers: The Bonds of Brotherhood ............ 5
Chapter 4: Behind Enemy Lines: Acts of Bravery ............ 7
Chapter 5: From Rookies to Veterans: The Evolution of Soldiers ............ 9
Chapter 6: Lasting Impressions: Memories of War ............ 11
Chapter 7: The Cost of Freedom: Lives Lost and Families Left Behind ............ 13
Chapter 8: A Different Kind of Courage: Women on the Frontline ............ 15
Chapter 9: The Enemy Within: Traitors and Spies ............ 17
Chapter 10: The Power of Faith: Religion in Times of War ............ 19
Chapter 11: The Aftermath: The Long Road Home ............ 21
Chapter 12: The Forgotten Frontlines: War in the Shadows ............ 23
Chapter 13: War in the Air: The Aces of Aviation ............ 25
Chapter 14: The Face of Evil: Confronting the Enemy ............ 27
Chapter 15: Injured but not Defeated: Soldiers' Stories of Survival ............ 29
Chapter 16: The Turning Point: Battles That Changed the Course of the War ............ 31
Chapter 17: From the Frontlines to Politics: War Veterans in Public Office ............ 33
Chapter 18: On the Brink of Death: Miraculous Escapes ............ 37
Chapter 19: The Heart of a Hero: Selflessness and Sacrifice ............ 39
Chapter 20: The Price of War: The Human Toll ............ 41
Chapter 21: Under Fire: The Art of Combat ............ 43
Chapter 22: A Nation Divided: War and Politics ............ 45
Chapter 23: The Courage to Lead: Officers and their Leadership Styles ............ 47
Chapter 24: A War on Two Fronts: The Struggle for Equality ............ 49
Chapter 25: The End of an Era: The Legacy of War ............ 51

Chapter 26: Heroes Among Us: Honoring Our Frontline Veterans................................................................................................. 53

# Chapter 1: The Call to Duty: Why They Served

The call to serve one's country in times of war has been answered by both men and women throughout the course of history. The motives behind their enlistment are as varied as the people who make up the armed forces, and can range from a sense of duty and patriotism to a yearning for adventure or the requirement of a stable job.

The choice to enlist in the military was a deeply personal one for many of the soldiers. They had a profound sense of allegiance to their nation, and they were convinced that it was their responsibility to protect it. Some were motivated to join the military by family members who had served in previous conflicts, while others felt compelled to carry on the legacy of their ancestors by serving in the military.

Others joined the military because they wanted to experience a sense of adventure and get the chance to travel and see the world during their time in service. They were excited to learn about new cultures and make connections with people from a variety of walks of life. They saw joining the military as an opportunity to increase the breadth of their perspectives and gain valuable experience in life.

A number of service members joined the military in order to get away from challenging situations back home. When times were tough economically or they couldn't find work, many people responded by enlisting in the military. The military provided the opportunity to have a secure job with consistent pay and benefits, in addition to the possibility of advancing one's career.

There was a sense of pride in their service and a willingness to put their lives in danger for their country that was common among all soldiers, regardless of the motivations that led them to join the military. They were aware that they would put themselves in harm's way and endure difficulties, but they were willing to do so in order to serve a greater cause.

A significant number of service members report that their time in the military had a profound impact on their lives. They became very close with the other soldiers in their unit, which contributed to the development of a strong sense of camaraderie. They gained experience in areas such as leadership, discipline, and collaboration that would be of great use to them in their post-military careers and civilian lives. They had a newfound appreciation for the rights and liberties that they had previously taken for granted. In addition, they had a newfound understanding of the value of the freedoms and privileges they had.

During times of war, the obligation to perform one's duties was especially pressing. Soldiers were well aware that their nation required them and that they were the only ones who could effectively defend their nation. They were ready to forsake their homes and the people they cared about most in order to serve their nation, even if it meant putting their own lives in danger.

In conclusion, the factors that influence a person's decision to answer the call to serve in the military are as varied as the person themselves. Soldiers are unified by their pride in their service to their country and their willingness to make sacrifices for the sake of their nation. This pride can be attributed to a sense of duty, a desire for adventure, or the need for a steady job. Those who answer the call to duty are among the bravest and most selfless members of our society. The call to duty is a powerful one.

# Chapter 2: In the Trenches: Surviving the Frontline

The frontline was a place fraught with danger, uncertainty, and a persistent threat for the soldiers who fought there. Soldiers serving in the trenches endured harsh conditions, including the risk of being shot by the enemy, being exposed to the elements, and the possibility of contracting a disease or infection. In order to survive, one needed to be mentally and physically strong, in addition to having a strong sense of camaraderie and working well with others.

In many instances, the living conditions in the trenches were arduous and uncomfortable. The conditions in which the soldiers were forced to sleep, which were often claustrophobic, damp, and lacking in ventilation, made them more susceptible to illness. They were frequently required to go for extended periods of time without having access to appropriate sanitation or hygiene facilities, which contributed to the spread of infections and illnesses.

The threat of being shot at by the enemy was one of the most significant hazards that frontline soldiers had to contend with. They were under constant threat of being attacked by artillery shells, grenades, and gunfire from the opposing forces. The constant awareness of the possibility of being attacked had a negative impact, not only on the physical health of the soldiers but also on their mental well-being. Being on the frontline was a constant source of stress and trauma for the soldiers, and as a result, many of them suffered from post-traumatic stress disorder as well as other mental health conditions.

It was also necessary to have a strong sense of camaraderie and to work together as a team in order to survive in the trenches. The emotional and physical well-being of a soldier was directly tied to his or her fellow service members. They became close with the other soldiers in their unit, which contributed to the improvement of their morale and helped them maintain a positive attitude.

In addition to the psychological and physiological difficulties, soldiers serving on the front lines were also forced to contend with the unpredictability and instability that are inherent to war. They had no way of knowing when or from where the next attack would come, so they were forced to remain on constant alert. Even the toughest soldiers could succumb to the effects of this level of anxiety and uncertainty, and many of them struggled to deal with the ever-present risk of being hurt or killed in battle.

The soldiers on the frontline remained dedicated to their mission and to one another in spite of the difficulties they faced. They were aware that their ability to collaborate effectively as a group was essential to their continued existence, and as a result, they were willing to make concessions for the sake of the greater good. The military experience provided many soldiers with a sense of purpose and meaning, and they were proud to be serving their country in such an important capacity during their time there.

In conclusion, surviving in the trenches was a challenging and dangerous task that required a combination of physical and mental toughness, in addition to a powerful sense of camaraderie and teamwork. The frontline soldiers were subjected to harsh conditions and lived in constant fear, but they never wavered in their dedication to their mission or to one another. Those who answer the call to duty do so because they are brave and selfless, and their service and sacrifice are a testament to those qualities.

# Chapter 3: A Band of Brothers: The Bonds of Brotherhood

The strong bonds of camaraderie that develop between service members during their time in the military are widely regarded as one of the defining aspects of military life. The sense of brotherhood and camaraderie that develops among soldiers is a potent force that can assist them in overcoming even the most difficult of obstacles.

Every day, soldiers collaborate closely with the other members of their unit in order to carry out their duties. They form a tight-knit community by working out together, eating together, and living together, which results in the group becoming like a second family to each other. They come to have profound feelings of trust and loyalty towards one another, and they are aware that they can depend on their fellow soldiers to have their backs regardless of the circumstances.

This sense of brotherhood is especially strong among soldiers who have served in the same unit during times of conflict. A connection that will last a lifetime can be forged between people through the shared experience of perceiving and overcoming peril and adversity. Soldiers who have been in the same battle together frequently refer to their fellow service members as their "brothers," and they often maintain close relationships with one another even after their time in the military has come to an end.

The emotional toll that military service can take on service members can be difficult to manage, but the bonds of brotherhood can help. Soldiers who are struggling with issues related to their mental health or with any other difficulties can seek support and understanding from their fellow soldiers. They are confident that they will not be stigmatized or judged for reaching out for assistance, and they are aware that their fellow service members will be there for them no matter what.

In addition to supplying emotional support, the bonds of brotherhood can also assist service members in maintaining their motivation and keeping their attention fixed on the mission at hand. Soldiers who have a strong sense of connection to the other members of their unit are more likely to take their responsibilities seriously and work diligently in order to achieve their objectives. They are also more likely to put their own needs aside in order to help their fellow soldiers because they are aware that their efforts will benefit the team as a whole. This is because they are aware that the team will benefit from their efforts.

The bonds of brotherhood are, in the eyes of many service members, among the most cherished and important aspects of their time spent in the armed forces. They often keep a strong sense of connection and camaraderie with one another throughout their lives and continue to maintain close relationships with their fellow soldiers long after their service has ended. These bonds are meant to serve as a reminder of the sacrifices that they made for their country, as well as the sense of purpose and meaning that they discovered in the act of serving their country.

To summarize, the bonds of brotherhood are a potent force that assist service members in overcoming the most difficult challenges that they face during their time in the armed forces. They offer emotional support, motivation, and a sense of belonging, all of which can be of great value to soldiers who are going through challenging circumstances. The sense of camaraderie and loyalty that develops among soldiers is a testament to the strength and resilience of the human spirit. It is also a source of inspiration and pride for all individuals who have served in the military.

# Chapter 4: Behind Enemy Lines: Acts of Bravery

Soldiers have been asked to participate in perilous and audacious operations behind enemy lines throughout the course of human history. These missions call for an exceptional level of bravery, skill, and ingenuity from the soldiers participating because they are required to navigate unfamiliar terrain, avoid detection by enemy forces, and complete their mission objectives with limited resources and support.

The invasion of Normandy on D-Day during World War II is widely regarded as one of the most notable examples of a mission that took place behind enemy lines. Behind enemy lines, Allied troops were parachuted in order to sabotage German defenses and interfere with their communications. These soldiers had to navigate terrain they were not familiar with, stay hidden from enemy patrols, and accomplish their missions all while being in constant danger of being discovered and ambushed.

Another well-known example of a mission that took place behind enemy lines was the assault on the prison camp at Son Tay in Vietnam. In the course of this mission, American soldiers were tasked with the mission of rescuing American prisoners of war who were being held in a prison camp that was extremely well fortified. In order for the soldiers to successfully complete their mission, they were required to navigate terrain that was unfamiliar to them, overcome significant obstacles, and engage in hand-to-hand combat with enemy forces.

Other types of missions that fall under the category of "behind enemy lines" include sabotage operations, reconnaissance missions, and search and rescue operations. In every instance, it was necessary for the soldiers to demonstrate an exceptionally high level of bravery as well as skill in order for them to successfully complete the objectives of their mission.

Missions that take place behind enemy lines require the soldiers to have a high level of skill as well as adaptability. They need to be able to think critically and make snap judgments when they are in potentially dangerous situations. They also need to have the ability to work effectively under pressure and when faced with unknown obstacles.

The soldiers who volunteer for these assignments do so willingly and with a great deal of pride, despite the fact that these missions are difficult and fraught with risk. They are well aware of the significance of their mission and the potential influence that their actions could have on the final outcome of the conflict.

The valor and selflessness shown by service members during these missions is a shining example of what can be expected from those who choose a career in the military. It serves as a poignant reminder of the hardships that service members are willing to endure in order to defend their nation and safeguard the safety of their fellow citizens.

In conclusion, missions that take place behind enemy lines are some of the most daring and dangerous missions that soldiers can undertake. They need to have an extraordinary amount of bravery, skill, and inventiveness in order to successfully complete the objectives of their mission. Soldiers who voluntarily participate in these missions do so willingly and with a great deal of pride because they are aware that their actions can have a significant influence on the overall course of the war. Their bravery and selflessness is a demonstration of the resiliency and strength of the human spirit, and it is a source of motivation and pride for all those who have served in the armed forces.

# Chapter 5: From Rookies to Veterans: The Evolution of Soldiers

During their time in the military, soldiers go through a significant personal development process. Every aspect of a soldier's life, from the time they sign up for basic training as untrained recruits until the time they leave active duty as grizzled veterans, requires them to grow and change in order to meet the demands of military service.

When people join the military for the first time, they frequently have no idea what will happen to them. They are put through strenuous training and are required to learn how to adjust to the rigid structure and discipline that is inherent in military life. In addition to this, they have to learn how to cooperate with others and carry out instructions without question.

The more a soldier serves in the military, the more experience and training they receive, as well as the more skills they learn. They become more self-assured and confident, and they improve their ability to deal with the challenges and uncertainties that come with a life in the military. In addition to this, they cultivate a stronger sense of loyalty and commitment to both their nation and the other soldiers in their unit.

One of the most significant changes that occur to a soldier's leadership abilities during their time in the military. The more experience a soldier has, the more responsibility he or she is given, and the greater the likelihood that they will be placed in a leadership role. They gain the ability to inspire their fellow soldiers to achieve their objectives by leading by setting a good example for them. They also learn how to make difficult choices under stress and how to accept responsibility for the results of their actions.

There have been significant shifts made to the manner in which soldiers are trained and equipped, in addition to the personal development that soldiers go through while serving their country. The training of soldiers has been significantly altered, as has the manner in which wars are fought, as a direct result of developments in both technology and strategy that have taken place in recent decades.

As an illustration, soldiers who served during World War I fought in trenches and relied on horses for transportation. On the other hand, soldiers participating in modern conflicts make use of cutting-edge weapons and vehicles and are outfitted with high-tech gear such as night vision goggles and body armor.

In spite of these shifts, the fundamental ideals and guidelines that guide military service have remained the same. In spite of the risks they face, soldiers are still expected to act bravely, loyally, and selflessly toward their comrades. They are still expected to work cooperatively as a group and to carry out instructions without raising any objections. They are still expected to give a significant amount of their time, energy, and resources in order to defend their nation and keep their fellow citizens safe.

To summarize, during their time in the military, service members go through a significant personal development process. They go from being inexperienced recruits to grizzled veterans as a result of gaining experience, acquiring new skills, and growing in self-assurance and self-reliance. The core values and principles of military service have not changed over the years, despite advances in technology and shifts in strategy. It is still expected of soldiers that they will demonstrate bravery, loyalty, and selflessness, and that they will make significant sacrifices for their country and the people who live in it. The evolution of soldiers is a testament to the strength and resilience of those who serve in the military, and it is a source of inspiration and pride for all those who have served in the armed forces in the past.

# Chapter 6: Lasting Impressions: Memories of War

War is a terrifying and life-altering experience that can make an indelible mark on those who have served their country in times of conflict. Wartime experiences have the potential to linger in the minds of former service members long after they have left the military, influencing their thoughts, feelings, and perspectives on life.

For many veterans, recollections of their time spent fighting in a conflict bring up a range of powerful feelings, including dread, rage, and melancholy. They may remember situations fraught with grave peril, the deaths of fellow service members, or the harrowing experience of bearing witness to acts of brutality and devastation. These memories have the potential to be overwhelming, which can lead to issues with mental health such as post-traumatic stress disorder and depression.

In spite of the difficulties that come along with wartime memories, these experiences can also serve as a wellspring of pride and motivation for veterans. They may remember instances of bravery and selflessness, times when they or their fellow soldiers put their lives in danger for the sake of a greater cause. They may also remember the sense of brotherhood and camaraderie that they experienced with the other soldiers in their unit, as well as the sense of purpose and meaning that they discovered in the service that they provided.

Wartime recollections have the potential to profoundly alter veterans' outlooks on life and its meaning. When soldiers return home from battle, they often have a deeper appreciation for the rights and responsibilities that come with being citizens of their respective countries. They may also have a heightened capacity for empathy and compassion for others who have been through traumatic experiences or difficult circumstances.

Wartime experiences have the potential to motivate some service members to continue serving their country in different capacities. They may decide to work as advocates for veterans' rights, pursue careers in fields such as law enforcement or public service, or work with organizations that provide support to military families.

Veterans typically are able to find ways to cope with the difficulties associated with wartime memories and continue living their lives, despite the fact that these memories can make it difficult for them to do so. They might go to a mental health professional for assistance in addressing their issues, or they might seek support from friends and family members instead. Connecting with other veterans and sharing their stories with those who have been through similar experiences can also provide them with a sense of solace and validation.

In conclusion, the experiences and recollections of war can have a significant and long-lasting effect on service members. They are often connected with powerful feelings such as dread and melancholy, but they also have the potential to serve as a wellspring of pride and motivation. Wartime experiences have the potential to mold veterans' perspectives on life and motivate them to continue serving their country in different capacities in the future. Soldiers are often able to find ways to cope with the difficulties associated with memories of war and to move on with their lives. The fact that they are able to do so is a testament to the strength and resilience of those who have served in the armed forces.

# Chapter 7: The Cost of Freedom: Lives Lost and Families Left Behind

The price of liberty is incalculable, and the efforts that soldiers put forth to defend their nation and the safety of their fellow citizens require a sizeable amount of self-sacrifice on their parts. One of the most significant drawbacks of serving in the military is the risk of losing one's life, as well as the anguish and disruption caused to the families who are forced to go on without their loved ones.

The passing of a family member or close friend while serving their country is a tragic event that can leave a mark on families for the rest of their lives. They not only have to deal with the emotional anguish and trauma of their loss, but also with the practical and financial repercussions that come along with the death of a family member. This might involve making preparations for a funeral, dealing with administrative tasks and legal issues, and adjusting to the loss of a source of income and financial support.

There are other people besides soldiers who can die while serving their country. Civilians who live in regions that are impacted by conflict are also at risk, and the loss of life has an impact not only on them but also on their families. This includes men, women, and children who are not participating in the conflict but are nonetheless unintentionally caught in the crossfire or who are purposefully targeted by hostile forces.

The soldiers and their families make significant sacrifices, and the effects of those sacrifices continue to reverberate long after the conflict has ended. Grief, anger, and guilt are common emotions that plague the families of those who have lost loved ones while serving their country. They may also find it difficult to come to terms with the fact that their loved one passed away due to the effects of a circumstance that they did not fully comprehend or endorse.

Despite the difficulties that come along with the loss of a loved one in the line of duty, military personnel and their families frequently find ways to cope with their grief and to pay tribute to the memory of their departed loved ones. This may include taking part in memorial services, establishing connections with other families who have been through a loss comparable to their own, or searching for ways to give back to their communities in recognition of the sacrifice made by their loved one.

A reminder of the true cost of freedom and the sacrifices that soldiers and their families make in order to defend their country and protect their fellow citizens is provided by the loss of life that occurs while serving one's country in the armed forces. It also serves as a reminder of how important it is to support military families and make certain that they have access to the resources and support they require in order to deal with the difficulties that come with living a life in the military.

In conclusion, one of the most significant expenses associated with military service is the loss of life while on active duty. Families who are left behind must come to terms not only with the emotional and psychological fallout of their loss, but also with the logistical and financial repercussions that come along with it. Despite the difficulties, soldiers and their families frequently discover ways to cope and to honor the memory of the people they have lost while serving in the military. Because of the sacrifices that soldiers and their families make, we are reminded of the real price that must be paid for freedom. It is imperative that we support military families and make certain that they have the resources and support they require in order to deal with the difficulties that come with living a military lifestyle.

# Chapter 8: A Different Kind of Courage: Women on the Frontline

Throughout the course of history, women have played an important part in the armed forces, most commonly serving in non-combat roles such as those of nurses and support staff. However, in recent years, women's roles in the military have expanded to include combat roles, such as serving as infantry soldiers and fighter pilots. Previously, women were only allowed to serve in non-combat roles in the military.

Women who serve in combat roles exhibit a distinct brand of bravery in comparison to their male counterparts who serve in the same capacity. They are required to not only be physically fit and proficient in combat, but also to be able to navigate the distinct obstacles and prejudices that they may face as women working in a field that is dominated by men.

Women who serve in combat roles are expected to be able to perform well under pressure, come to decisions quickly, and collaborate effectively with their fellow service members. In addition to this, they should be able to adjust to shifting conditions and respond with self-assurance and professionalism when confronted with unforeseen challenges.

In addition to these abilities, women who serve in combat roles need to be mentally and physically ready to take on specific challenges that their male counterparts may not have to deal with. They may have to contend with discrimination or harassment at the hands of other service members, or they may have trouble locating suitable accommodations for personal hygiene and privacy.

In spite of the difficulties they face, the women who serve in combat roles have demonstrated extraordinary bravery and determination. They have demonstrated to their fellow soldiers that they are capable soldiers who are also skilled, and as a result, they have earned the respect and admiration of their peers.

It is a significant advance toward gender equality and for the advancement of the military as a whole that women are now allowed to serve in combat roles. This demonstrates that women are just as capable as men when it comes to defending the rights of their fellow citizens and serving their country in a military capacity.

However, there is still much work to be done in order to guarantee that women are fully integrated into combat roles and are provided with the support and resources that they require in order to be successful. This includes addressing issues of discrimination and harassment, as well as providing women in combat roles with the appropriate accommodations and resources.

In conclusion, women who serve in combat roles exhibit a distinct kind of bravery in comparison to their male counterparts who serve in the same capacity. In addition to displaying the necessary physical and mental abilities, they are expected to navigate the particular obstacles and prejudices that they face as women working in a field that is primarily dominated by men. There has been significant progress made toward gender equality and for the military as a whole with the introduction of women serving in combat roles; however, there is still much work to be done to ensure that women serving in these roles are fully integrated and supported in their roles. Women who serve in combat roles are a testament to the strength and resiliency of women, and they serve as an inspiration to all individuals who are courageous enough to serve their country.

# Chapter 9: The Enemy Within: Traitors and Spies

Throughout history, military forces have had to contend with the possibility that members of their own ranks may be spies or traitors. These people could be driven by a wide range of considerations, such as financial gain, ideological commitment, or personal ambition.

Spies and traitors can be a significant threat to military operations because they may divulge sensitive information to hostile forces or sabotage essential infrastructure and equipment. They have the potential to lower the morale of the soldiers and erode their trust in one another, both of which can have a negative influence on the cohesiveness and efficiency of the unit.

Benedict Arnold, who is known for betraying the American forces while they were fighting in the Revolutionary War, is considered to be one of the most infamous examples of a traitor in the annals of military history. Arnold was a well-respected general in the Continental Army, but his actions were driven by a desire for personal gain and recognition. In exchange for money and a position in the British army, he devised a plan to collaborate with the British in order to hand over the strategically significant fort located at West Point in New York.

Both the Cambridge Five, a group of British intelligence agents who were recruited by the Soviet Union during the Cold War, and Robert Hanssen, an FBI agent who was convicted of spying for the Russian government, are additional examples of traitors and spies. The Cambridge Five were British intelligence agents who were recruited by the Soviet Union.

Military forces are constantly concerned about the possibility of betrayal and espionage, and soldiers are trained to be vigilant for signs of suspicious behavior or activities in order to detect potential threats. Soldiers are encouraged to report any suspicious behavior or activities to their superiors, as military intelligence units work to identify and neutralize potential threats. Additionally, soldiers are encouraged to report any suspicious behavior or activities to their peers.

In spite of the fact that traitors and spies pose a risk, military forces have devised a wide range of strategies and methods to reduce the likelihood that these risks will materialize. This includes carrying out exhaustive background checks on personnel, enforcing stringent security protocols, and carrying out routine counterintelligence operations.

To summarize, there is always cause for concern regarding the possibility of spies and traitors operating within armed forces. These individuals have the potential to cause significant harm to military operations, as well as to the morale of the troops and their trust in one another. However, in order to reduce the risk posed by these dangers, the armed forces have developed a wide range of strategies and strategies, and soldiers are also trained to be on the lookout for any indicators that could point to suspicious behavior or activities. The ongoing fight against traitors and spies is a testament to the resiliency and dedication of those who serve in the military. It also serves as a reminder of the significance of remaining vigilant and committed to one's role in the defense of one's country.

# Chapter 10: The Power of Faith: Religion in Times of War

Religion has played an important part throughout the history of warfare, with many soldiers and military leaders drawing on their beliefs to find the fortitude and bravery they need to fight during times of conflict. Religion has also played a role in the formation of military strategy, as well as in the process of providing soldiers and their families with solace and support.

A great number of service members draw strength and solace from their religious beliefs. They may turn to prayer or religious rituals in order to find the strength and courage to face the danger that they face, or in order to deal with the trauma and stress that comes with serving in the military. A sense of purpose and meaning can also be provided by faith, which can assist service members in developing a more profound sense of connection to their fellow service members and to their country.

Religion has also played a part in the development of military strategy and the progression of wars and conflicts throughout history. From the Crusades to the conflict between Israelis and Palestinians, religious differences have been at the root of many wars and conflicts throughout the course of history. Religious leaders have played a role in shaping public opinion and in advocating for peace or conflict throughout history. Religious leaders have also frequently used religious rhetoric in order to motivate their troops and to justify the actions that they have taken.

Religion has played a significant role not only in the development of military strategy but also in the provision of solace and support to those serving in the armed forces. Chaplains and other religious leaders are frequently present on military bases and in the field to provide soldiers of all faiths with spiritual guidance and support. They may also offer more tangible assistance, such as assisting service members in the organization of religious services or in the acquisition of religious literature.

There are many obstacles to overcome when it comes to the intersection of religion and war, despite the fact that religion can play a positive role in the service of those who choose to join the armed forces. Religious rhetoric can be used to justify acts of violence and aggression, which can lead to tension and conflict among soldiers. Different religious beliefs and practices can lead to tension and conflict among soldiers.

Additionally, there is a possibility that one's religious beliefs could be utilized or manipulated for the purpose of gaining political advantage, which could result in conflict and division. It is essential for members of the armed forces and their leaders to be aware of these dangers and to make efforts to foster religious tolerance and understanding among service members who adhere to a variety of faiths.

In conclusion, religion has played an important part throughout the annals of military history as well as in the lives of those who have served. It has the potential to offer solace and assistance during times of conflict, to help shape military strategy, and to offer spiritual guidance and assistance to service members of all faiths. However, there are also challenges associated with the intersection of religion and war, including the potential for conflict and tension among soldiers of different faiths in a given conflict. The power of faith in times of war is a testament to the resiliency and strength of the human spirit. It also serves as a reminder of the significance of discovering meaning and purpose in one's life, regardless of how challenging the circumstances may be.

# Chapter 11: The Aftermath: The Long Road Home

Soldiers and their families often find the transition back to civilian life after serving in the military to be a trying and emotional experience. The readjustment to civilian life can be challenging, and returning service members may have trouble adapting to the alterations and difficulties that come with their new lives.

The mental and emotional toll that serving one's country can take can be one of the most difficult obstacles for a veteran to overcome upon returning home. It can be challenging for many veterans to readjust to civilian life because of mental health conditions such as post-traumatic stress disorder (PTSD), depression, and anxiety. It's possible that they struggle with feelings of isolation, guilt, and anger, and that they find it challenging to get back in touch with their families and friends.

Finding work, securing housing, and gaining access to healthcare are just some of the potential logistical obstacles that service members may face upon returning home, in addition to the emotional challenges that accompany this transition. It may be necessary to have a significant amount of support and resources available in order to overcome these challenges, which can be particularly severe for soldiers who were injured or disabled while serving in the military.

In spite of these obstacles, service members can frequently find ways to cope with their experiences and make a successful transition back to civilian life. This may include seeking professional help for issues related to mental health, connecting with other veterans and support organizations for the military, and pursuing opportunities for education or job training.

During this time, having the support of family and friends is essential to helping ease the transition back into civilian life. It's possible that soldiers need assistance getting back in touch with their families and repairing any relationships that were damaged while they were serving in the military. They may also need assistance adjusting to the logistical challenges of civilian life, such as managing their finances and figuring out the healthcare system, which are both new to them.

In addition to these challenges on an individual level, the readjustment to civilian life also has repercussions that are more widespread for society as a whole. Veterans enter the civilian workforce with a set of distinct abilities and experiences, and their contributions can be extremely beneficial to both the economy and the communities in which they live. However, there is frequently a gap between the skills and experiences that soldiers gain while serving in the armed forces and the opportunities that are open to them when they return to civilian life. Not only will addressing this issue and making certain that veterans have access to the resources and support they require for success be of benefit to veterans, but it will also be of benefit to their families, communities, and the nation as a whole.

In conclusion, returning to civilian life after serving in the military can be a trying and emotional experience for both the service member and his or her family. The emotional toll of military service, in addition to the practical difficulties of finding employment and gaining access to healthcare, can make it challenging for veterans to readjust to life in civilian society. However, with the assistance of support from family and friends, access to professional resources, and opportunities for education and job training, many soldiers are able to find ways to cope and successfully transition back to civilian life. Not only the veterans themselves, but also their families, communities, and the nation as a whole stand to gain from efforts made to ensure that veterans have access to the resources and support they require in order to be successful in their endeavors.

# Chapter 12: The Forgotten Frontlines: War in the Shadows

Although most wars are fought on open battlefields with defined lines of engagement, there are also a great number of conflicts that take place in the shadows. These wars are fought by special operations forces, intelligence agencies, and other organizations that operate behind enemy lines and, most of the time, in complete secrecy.

These so-called "shadow wars" are fought for a variety of reasons, some of which include the collection of intelligence, the disruption of enemy operations, and the execution of targeted strikes against high-value targets. Small teams of highly trained and skilled operatives are typically responsible for carrying them out. These operations can involve a wide variety of strategies, ranging from clandestine surveillance to targeted assassinations.

The drone program of the United States, which has been used to carry out targeted strikes against high-value targets in countries such as Pakistan, Yemen, and Somalia, is one of the most well-known examples of a shadow war. It is also one of the most controversial examples of a shadow war. Supporters of the program argue that it is an essential instrument in the fight against terrorism, despite the fact that it has been met with widespread opposition.

Other examples of shadow wars include the activities of special operations forces such as the Navy SEALs and Delta Force. These forces operate covertly and frequently carry out high-risk missions such as the capture or elimination of high-value targets and the rescue of hostages.

Shadow wars are often overlooked and underreported by both the media and the general public, despite the fact that they play an important role in today's modern military conflicts. This is because of the secrecy that surrounds these operations, as well as the fact that they frequently take place in remote areas, away from traditional battlegrounds, and have less obvious effects on the civilian populations in the areas they are conducted in.

However, shadow wars can have a significant impact, not only in terms of the importance they have from a strategic standpoint but also in terms of the effect they have on the soldiers who fight in them. The secrecy and the high level of danger involved in these operations can take a toll on the mental and emotional health of the soldiers involved, and they can also give rise to ethical conundrums and moral worries.

In conclusion, shadow wars are an essential component of modern military conflicts; however, the media and the general public frequently fail to recognize their significance and underreport their occurrence. These wars are fought by operatives who are highly skilled and trained and who operate behind enemy lines and often in secret. These wars can involve a variety of strategies, from covert surveillance to targeted strikes, and are fought by highly skilled and trained operatives. In spite of the fact that these operations are extremely important from a strategic standpoint, the fact that they are conducted in secret and involve a high level of risk can take a toll on the mental and emotional health of the soldiers involved. It can also lead to ethical conundrums and moral concerns. It is important for the public to be aware of the role that shadow wars play in modern military conflicts and to recognize the sacrifices made by the soldiers who carry them out. It is also important for the public to be aware of the sacrifices made by the soldiers who carry out these shadow wars.

# Chapter 13: War in the Air: The Aces of Aviation

The advent of new aviation technology completely altered the nature of armed conflict by providing militaries with a fresh viewpoint of the battleground and making it possible to launch aerial assaults and conduct reconnaissance from above. A new kind of warrior, known as an ace of aviation, emerged alongside the development of aviation technology.

Aces were fighter pilots who served during World Wars I and II and had a record of five or more victories in dogfighting against enemy aircraft. They were the best of the best, with extraordinary flying skills and a profound understanding of aerial tactics and strategy. They were the elite of the elite.

Aces enjoyed a high level of respect among their peers as well as among the senior leaders of the armed forces, and they were frequently called upon to participate in dangerous missions or to instruct new pilots. Their exploits were celebrated in the media and in popular culture, and as a result, many of them became well-known names in the general public.

One of the most well-known flying aces of all time was Manfred von Richthofen, also known as the "Red Baron." Richthofen was a German fighter pilot who served during World War I. He is credited with 80 victories in the air during that conflict. He was a hero in Germany due to his innovative tactics and the exceptional flying skills he possessed, which earned him that title.

Eddie Rickenbacker, an American pilot who distinguished himself as a leading ace during World War I, and Saburo Sakai, a Japanese ace who served in the Pacific theater of World War II, are two examples of other notable aces in the history of aviation.

Aces of the sky had to brave significant dangers and overcome difficult obstacles, despite their bravery and skill. The aerial combat that took place during World Wars I and II was extremely hazardous, and the pilots who participated did so under the constant threat of being injured or killed. In addition to this, they had to contend with the mental and physical strains that came with flying, such as the extreme cold, the lack of oxygen, and the mental toll that being in combat took on them.

Aces of aviation played an important part in military conflicts that occurred in the 20th century, and their contributions helped to shape the paths that these conflicts took. Despite the difficulties they faced, they were able to make a significant contribution. Their bravery, talent, and commitment continue to serve as a source of motivation for up-and-coming generations of pilots and military personnel.

As a conclusion, aces of aviation played a significant part in the military conflicts that occurred in the 20th century. They were able to achieve victories in air-to-air combat by utilizing their exceptional flying skills as well as their understanding of aerial tactics and strategy. Aces of aviation were highly respected and celebrated by their fellow pilots as well as by military leaders for their contributions, which helped to shape the course of these conflicts. This was the case despite the dangers and difficulties they faced in the course of their careers. Their bravery and commitment continue to serve as a source of motivation for future generations of military pilots and personnel, and they are a useful reminder of the power and significance of aviation technology in today's modern conflicts.

# Chapter 14: The Face of Evil: Confronting the Enemy

In times of armed conflict, it is common for soldiers to be put in the precarious position of having to face their adversaries. This may involve engaging the enemy in combat, launching targeted strikes, or gathering intelligence on the activities and operations of the adversary.

Soldiers may experience a wide range of feelings, ranging from anger and hatred to fear and compassion, when they are forced to confront the enemy. This can be a deeply emotional and psychologically taxing experience for them. In addition to this, it can be physically hazardous, putting the soldiers in constant danger of being hurt or killed in some way.

Confronting the adversary, on the other hand, is an essential component of military conflict and can be absolutely necessary for achieving victory and ensuring the safety of both military personnel and civilians. Soldiers are able to foil the enemy's plans and prevent them from carrying out attacks if they gather intelligence regarding the activities and operations of the adversary. Soldiers are able to neutralize the capabilities of the enemy and protect their own forces as well as civilians by participating in combat.

Confronting the enemy, despite the fact that it is important, can also be a complicated issue from a moral and ethical standpoint. It is possible for soldiers to be put in a position where they must make difficult choices, such as whether or not to use deadly force against an enemy combatant or whether or not to take prisoners of war. They may also be put in situations in which the enemy is not clearly defined, such as when they are engaged in conflicts with non-state actors or when they are engaged in operations to counter insurgency.

In addition, when it comes to identifying the enemy, the soldiers may have a difficult time doing so. It is possible for soldiers to struggle with feelings of hatred or prejudice when they are fighting in conflicts in which the enemy is defined by factors such as race, ethnicity, or religion. It is essential for members of the armed forces and those in positions of authority within the military to be aware of these difficulties and to make efforts to encourage ethical and moral conduct among service members.

In conclusion, engaging in combat with the adversary is an essential component of armed conflict, and it can be absolutely necessary for achieving victory and ensuring the safety of both military personnel and civilians. In addition to being difficult on a mental, emotional, and psychological level, it may also bring up difficult moral and ethical questions. Soldiers and military leaders need to be aware of these challenges and work to promote ethical and moral behavior among other soldiers. At the same time, they need to recognize the importance of confronting the enemy in order to achieve strategic objectives and protect those who are under their care.

# Chapter 15: Injured but not Defeated: Soldiers' Stories of Survival

During times of armed conflict, there is always the possibility that a service member will suffer an injury or become disabled. Soldiers may be left with physical or mental scars that can have a long-lasting impact on their lives, regardless of whether the scars were caused by injuries sustained in combat, accidents, or illnesses.

Many injured service members are able to find ways to overcome the obstacles presented by their injuries and continue to lead fulfilling lives, which is a testament to the resilience of the human spirit. These soldiers are frequently a source of motivation for others because they illustrate how the human spirit can remain resilient and strong in the face of adversity.

Tammy Duckworth, a senator from the United States and a former officer in the Army National Guard, is a good example of a soldier who overcame her injuries despite the fact that she lost both of her legs while serving in Iraq. In spite of the injuries she sustained, Duckworth went on to complete her doctoral degree, run for Congress, and eventually become a senator for the United States. Her life serves as a powerful example of what can be accomplished when one is determined and resilient.

Another illustration is that of Sergeant Brendan Marrocco, a veteran of the United States Army who was amputated on all four of his limbs while serving in Iraq. Marrocco has gone on to have a successful career as a musician and an artist, and he has even learned how to drive a car utilizing a special prosthetic device. This is all in spite of the injuries he sustained. His story serves as a powerful example of the importance of adjusting well to changes in one's environment and discovering ways to thrive despite the obstacles presented by an injury or disability.

In addition to suffering from physical wounds, soldiers are at an increased risk of developing mental health conditions such as post-traumatic stress disorder (PTSD), depression, and anxiety. These problems can be just as debilitating as physical injuries, and overcoming them may require a significant amount of support and resources.

Many service members are able to find ways to cope with the difficulties of injury and disability and go on to lead lives that are meaningful and rewarding despite these obstacles. This may include seeking professional help for issues relating to physical or mental health, pursuing opportunities for education or job training, or connecting with other veterans and organizations that provide support for the military.

In conclusion, veterans who have been injured or disabled as a result of their service in the armed forces are frequently able to find ways to overcome their injuries and continue to lead lives that are meaningful to them. Their accounts of fortitude and tenacity in the face of adversity serve both as a source of motivation for those who hear them and as a timely reminder of the strength of the human spirit. It is important for soldiers to receive the support and resources that they need in order to cope with injury and disability. Additionally, it is important for society as a whole to acknowledge the sacrifices made by these soldiers and to honor their contributions to our country.

# Chapter 16: The Turning Point: Battles That Changed the Course of the War

In each and every military conflict, there are decisive battles that play a major role in determining the overall outcome of the conflict. These skirmishes are frequently the junctures at which the tide of the conflict turns in favor of one of the contending parties rather than the other.

The Battle of Stalingrad during World War II is a good example of a battle that marked a turning point in the war. It was one of the bloodiest battles of the war, and it was fought between German and Soviet forces for control of the city of Stalingrad. The battle was one of the bloodiest battles. The Soviet forces were successful in driving back the German troops and ultimately achieving victory after a period of months of intense fighting. It is generally agreed that the battle marked the first significant loss for the German army and shifted the momentum in favor of the Allies. As a result, the battle is regarded as a turning point in the war.

One more illustration of this can be found in the Battle of Midway that took place during World War II. The conflict took place in the Pacific theater between the United States and Japan, and the result was a decisive victory for the United States Navy in the conflict. The battle was the first significant loss for the Japanese navy, and it stopped Japan from expanding its reach in the Pacific as a result of the conflict. It is generally agreed upon that the battle was a defining moment in the course of the war because it swung the balance of power in favor of the Allies in the Pacific theater.

In addition to the examples given above, there have been a great number of other engagements throughout history that have significantly altered the path that military conflicts have taken. It's possible that these battles were won by employing superior strategies or tactics, but more likely, they were won by sheer force of will and determination.

Not only on the battlefield, but also in the larger political and social context of a conflict, turning point battles can have a significant impact on the outcome of the conflict. They have the ability to shift public opinion, alter the priorities of strategic planning, and even change the distribution of power between nations.

In conclusion, battles that mark a turning point in the course of a conflict are an essential component of armed conflicts and have a significant influence on the results of wars. They can be won by employing superior tactics or strategies, as well as by using sheer force of will and determination. The results of these battles can not only be felt on the battlefield, but also in the larger political and social context of a conflict, and they have the potential to alter the overall direction that history takes. It is vital to investigate and comprehend these conflicts in order to acquire a more profound appreciation for the efforts put forth by soldiers and to acknowledge the significance of their contributions to our nation as well as to the rest of the world.

# Chapter 17: From the Frontlines to Politics: War Veterans in Public Office

Veterans of past wars have consistently been influential figures in politics and other areas of public service throughout history. A great number of former service members have gone on to successful careers in politics, both as candidates and as elected officials at all levels of government, drawing on their prior experience in the military as well as their proven leadership abilities.

George H.W. Bush is a good example of this because he was a pilot during World War II and then went on to become a congressman, director of the CIA, vice president, and eventually president of the United States. It is generally agreed upon that George W. Bush is one of the most capable and experienced leaders in the annals of modern American history. Bush's leadership style and approach to foreign policy were both significantly influenced by his time spent serving in the military.

Tammy Duckworth, a member of the United States Senate and a former officer in the Army National Guard, is another example. Duckworth was wounded in Iraq and lost both of her legs during the conflict there. Her time spent serving in the military has been a significant factor in shaping Duckworth's views on a variety of issues, including veterans' rights and military policy, as they pertain to her political career. She has been a vociferous advocate for veterans and their families, and she has worked to expand veterans' access to medical care and other resources that are available to those who have served in the military of our country.

There are a great number of other war veterans who, like Bush and Duckworth, have made significant contributions to politics as well as other areas of public service. These veterans bring a fresh viewpoint to their positions in government, with a profound comprehension of the hardships endured by soldiers and a dedication to meeting the requirements of veterans and the families of those who have served.

However, veterans who are active in politics face additional unique difficulties and challenges. It's possible that they'll have trouble adjusting to the pace and culture of government work, or that they'll encounter resistance from those who doubt their capacity to lead in settings that aren't related to the military. It may be challenging for veterans to navigate the demands of public service if they are coping with mental health issues such as post-traumatic stress disorder (PTSD) or depression.

Veterans who enter politics have the potential to make a significant impact on both our society and the world, in spite of the obstacles that stand in their way. They bring a fresh point of view to the discussion, along with a profound comprehension of the hardships endured by service members and a dedication to meeting the requirements of veterans and the people who care for them. It is critical that our culture acknowledges the value that veterans bring to the political process and provides them with encouragement and assistance as they pursue opportunities to continue serving their country in this capacity.

In conclusion, throughout the course of history, veterans of war have played a significant role in politics and public service, utilizing their prior experience in the military in addition to their skills as leaders in order to pursue careers in various levels of government. They bring a fresh viewpoint to their positions in government, with a profound comprehension of the hardships endured by service members and a dedication to meeting the requirements of veterans and the people who care for them. Veterans who enter politics face a potentially unique set of challenges and roadblocks, but they also have the opportunity to have a significant influence on both our society and the world. It is critical that our culture acknowledges the value that veterans bring to the political process and provides them with encouragement and assistance as they pursue opportunities to continue serving their country in this capacity.

# Chapter 18: On the Brink of Death: Miraculous Escapes

When participating in armed conflict, soldiers frequently put themselves in situations where death is a very real possibility. However, there are some soldiers who are able to defy death and survive despite the overwhelming odds against them by overcoming incredible obstacles and making miraculous escapes.

One example of this is the story of Douglas Bader, a British fighter pilot who was involved in an accident that occurred before the start of World War II and caused him to lose both of his legs. Bader was determined to fly again despite the injuries he sustained, and as a result, he went on to become one of the most skilled fighter pilots in the Royal Air Force during the war. He was eventually brought down by hostile fire over enemy territory and taken prisoner, but he managed to break free from their custody and make his way back to England. The story of Bader is illustrative of the power that can be harnessed through determination and the will to survive.

Another illustration of this can be found in the story of Aron Ralston, a hiker from the United States who became entombed beneath a boulder while he was hiking in Utah. After going five days without eating or drinking anything, Ralston was finally forced to amputate his own arm in order to free himself and make his way to safety. The story of Ralston serves as a powerful illustration of the incredible strength of the human spirit, even in the face of the gravest of adversities.

In addition to the examples given here, there are a great number of other accounts of soldiers and civilians who, during times of war, made miraculous comebacks from the brink of death. These tales are meant to serve as a cautionary reminder of the precarious nature of life as well as the strength of the human will to endure adversity.

Having said that, it is essential that we acknowledge the toll that going through such an experience can have on an individual. Those who survive traumatic experiences may struggle with a variety of physical and mental health issues, such as post-traumatic stress disorder (PTSD), anxiety, and depression. It is essential for people who have been through something similar to look for support and resources that will assist them in making sense of what has happened to them and moving forward in a way that is both healthy and constructive.

In conclusion, accounts of people who miraculously evaded death during times of conflict serve as a potent reminder of the resiliency of the human spirit and the will to survive. These accounts are illustrative of the power of determination and the capacity of individuals to triumph despite the most insurmountable of obstacles. It is essential, despite this fact, to acknowledge the toll that such experiences can take on individuals and to provide support and resources in order to assist survivors in coping with their experiences and moving forward in a way that is both healthy and positive.

# Chapter 19: The Heart of a Hero: Selflessness and Sacrifice

An unwavering sense of selflessness and the willingness to make a sacrifice lies at the center of every heroic act. Acts of heroism are characterized by a willingness to put the requirements of others ahead of one's own, whether it be a soldier giving their life for their country, a civilian risking their safety to help others, or a first responder rushing into danger to save lives. This willingness to put the requirements of others ahead of one's own is what makes a hero.

One story that illustrates the meaning of the word "hero" is that of Sergeant First Class Alwyn Cashe, who served in the United States Army and was killed in Iraq while attempting to save his fellow soldiers from a burning vehicle. Cashe refused to seek medical attention for himself despite the fact that he had suffered severe burns and other injuries until all of his fellow soldiers had been rescued. The power of sacrifice and the willingness to put others before oneself is demonstrated by the brave act that he performed without regard for his own safety.

The story of Rick Rescorla, a veteran of the Vietnam War who was working as the chief of security at the World Trade Center on 9/11, is another illustration of this phenomenon. It is believed that Rescorla was responsible for saving the lives of thousands of people on that fateful day by guiding them to safety prior to the collapse of the towers. Although Rescorla did not make it through the assaults himself, his bravery and selflessness in the face of danger serve as a powerful example of the transformative potential of making a sacrifice.

In addition to the aforementioned instances, there are innumerable other tales of heroism and selflessness that have taken place during times of conflict as well as times of relative peace. These accounts enlighten us and serve as a powerful reminder of the extraordinary capacity of human beings to behave courageously and altruistically when confronted with peril.

However, it is essential to be aware that heroic deeds frequently involve taking risks that can result in significant losses. Those who engage in heroic deeds run the risk of being hurt or even killed in the process, leaving behind families and loved ones. It is important for society to recognize and honor the sacrifices made by these individuals, and it is also important for society to provide support and resources for the families and loved ones of the individuals who have performed heroic acts as a result of their heroic acts.

In conclusion, heroic deeds are defined by a willingness to prioritize the requirements of others over one's own, and they are a demonstration of the efficacy of giving up one's own interests in favor of those of others. These deeds can take place during times of conflict or peace, and they motivate us to be the best versions of ourselves and to work toward making the world a better place. In spite of this, it is necessary to acknowledge and honor the sacrifices made by those who perform heroic deeds, as well as to offer support and resources to the families and loved ones of those individuals after the heroic deeds they have performed have been carried out.

# Chapter 20: The Price of War: The Human Toll

The cost in human life caused by war is incalculable. The physical, emotional, and psychological effects of war have varying degrees of an impact on different people, including military personnel, civilians, and families. The human toll is the true staggering cost of war, despite the fact that the cost of war is frequently measured in terms of dollars and resources.

The physical toll that war takes on soldiers is one example of the human toll that war exacts. In the heat of battle, soldiers run the risk of being hurt or even killed, leaving their families and loved ones to mourn their loss. Those who make it through the ordeal may be left with permanent injuries or disabilities as a result of their ordeal, depending on the severity.

One more illustration of this is the mental toll taken on both military personnel and civilians. Exposure to the stress and dangers of war can often lead to a variety of mental health problems, including post-traumatic stress disorder (PTSD), anxiety, and depression. These problems can be incapacitating, having an effect not only on the individual but also on their families and the people they care about the most.

War not only has a significant impact on individuals, but also on communities and societies as a whole. This is in addition to the personal toll that it takes. It is possible for the destruction of homes, infrastructure, and cultural sites to have an enduring effect on the social fabric of a society, leaving behind wounds that may not completely heal for several generations.

It is essential for society to acknowledge the human cost of war and to offer support and resources to those whose lives have been altered by it. Access to healthcare, mental health services, and other resources that can assist individuals and communities in coping with the aftereffects of war may be included in this definition.

In conclusion, the human toll that war exacts is staggering and has a wide-ranging impact on people on an individual level as well as their families and communities. The cost of war is frequently measured in terms of dollars and resources; however, the human toll is the only thing that can truly be measured. It is important for society to recognize the impact that war has on individuals and communities, and it is equally important for society to provide support and resources to help individuals and communities cope with the physical, emotional, and psychological effects of war.

# Chapter 21: Under Fire: The Art of Combat

Combat is an art form that requires talent, self-control, and concentration. Soldiers are required to be able to react rapidly and decisively in the face of potential danger, relying on both their training and their innate abilities to prevail over their adversaries.

The ability to maintain situational awareness, also known as an understanding of one's surroundings and the movements of the enemy, is one of the most important aspects of combat. This calls for a combination of skills, including observation, the gathering of intelligence, and the ability to make snap decisions.

The ability to collaborate successfully with one's allies is another essential quality for a combatant to possess. In order for soldiers to achieve a common objective, they need to be able to effectively communicate with one another and coordinate their movements and actions. For this to work, there must be mutual respect, trust, and an in-depth comprehension of each other's capabilities and limitations.

In addition to these skills, combat requires mental and physical toughness in order to be successful. Soldiers need to be able to withstand the strenuous physical demands of combat, which include working long hours, being exposed to hostile environments, and facing the possibility of being hurt or killed. They need to be able to cope with the psychological stresses of combat, such as the trauma of witnessing violence and the fear of their own mortality. They need to be able to do this in order to be successful.

The art of combat relies heavily on training and preparation on the part of its practitioners. In order to be adequately prepared for battle, soldiers must first endure strenuous mental and physical training, which may include training in the use of various weapons, hand-to-hand combat, and survival skills. They are also required to have the mental fortitude to withstand the rigors of combat, which includes the possibility of being hurt or killed.

In conclusion, the art of combat is one that requires not only skill but also discipline and concentration. Soldiers are required to be able to demonstrate mental and physical toughness, continue to maintain situational awareness, and work effectively as part of a team. Training and preparation are essential aspects of the art of combat, and soldiers need to be able to rely on both their training and their instincts in order to react rapidly and decisively in the face of potential danger. To be successful in the art of combat, soldiers need to draw on their mental, physical, and emotional reserves. This is because the art of combat is a complex and difficult field.

# Chapter 22: A Nation Divided: War and Politics

War has the potential to drive a wedge between nations, as various factions and political groups within a nation may hold opposing views on the reasons for going to war, the strategies employed during conflict, and the desired outcomes of the war. Additionally, war frequently has significant economic, social, and cultural impacts, which can further exacerbate existing divisions within a society. This is because these facets of war's aftermath are often interconnected.

The American Civil War is a good example of a war that tore a nation apart, as it pitted the Union against the Confederacy in a conflict that was fought over the issue of slavery as well as the rights of individual states. The war was responsible for a significant amount of political, economic, and social upheaval, which led to the eventual abolition of slavery. However, it also left behind deep scars and divisions that wouldn't begin to heal for decades after the war was over.

One more illustration is the United States' involvement in the Vietnam War, which was met with widespread opposition and contributed to the country's increasing political polarization. There were significant rifts within American society as a result of the fact that many Americans held opposing views regarding the reasons for going to war and the strategies used by the United States military.

In addition to the examples given above, there have been a plethora of other wars that have caused nations and societies to become deeply divided. It is essential to acknowledge the impact that war has on politics and to make efforts to identify areas of agreement and find solutions that can help to bridge the divides that exist between the various groups and factions.

It is important for individuals and communities to engage in open and honest dialogue in order to address the impact that war has on politics. Individuals and communities should work toward greater understanding and empathy for different points of view, and they should look for common ground wherever it is possible. In order to achieve this goal, it may be necessary to reach out across political, social, and cultural divides and work toward the discovery of solutions that are in the best interests of all members of society.

It is important for individuals and communities to recognize the impact that war has on politics and to work towards finding common ground and solutions that can bridge the gaps between different groups and factions. In conclusion, war has the power to divide nations and societies, leading to political polarization, economic disruption, and social upheaval. It is possible that the wounds caused by war can be healed by having conversations that are open and honest, as well as by making a commitment to empathy and understanding. This would be a step toward a more united and peaceful future.

# Chapter 23: The Courage to Lead: Officers and their Leadership Styles

During times of conflict, officers play an essential part in guiding and motivating soldiers to accomplish their objectives and achieve success on the battlefield. However, different officers may have different approaches to leadership, and the efficiency with which they lead can have a significant bearing on the level of success that is achieved by military operations.

General George S. Patton is a good example of a successful military leader. He was known for his aggressive and charismatic leadership style during his time in the military. Patton was unafraid to take risks and make courageous choices in order to accomplish the goals he set for himself. He was also a firm believer in leading from the front. His soldiers looked up to him as a powerful and motivational figure, and as a result, they showed him a great deal of respect.

Another illustration of this is Admiral William H. McRaven, who presided over the United States Special Operations Command and was in charge of some of the military operations that received the most media attention over the course of the past two decades. McRaven is well-known for his ability to inspire and motivate his troops to achieve their goals, as well as for his leadership style, which is characterized by calmness and analytical thinking. He emphasized the significance of being prepared, working together as a team, and maintaining discipline in order to be successful on the battlefield.

In addition to the examples given here, there are a large number of other military leaders who have shown bravery, determination, and the ability to lead effectively during times of conflict. It is essential to acknowledge the influence that leadership has on military operations and to educate oneself on the various leadership approaches and strategies that can be utilized to achieve success on the battlefield.

To be an effective military leader, one must possess a variety of skills, such as the ability to communicate clearly, the aptitude to formulate tactical plans while under duress, and the capacity to instill confidence in and encourage one's subordinates. In addition to this, you need to have a comprehensive understanding of the military mission as well as the goals that need to be accomplished.

To summarize, officers play an essential part in guiding soldiers to victory on the battlefield, and different officers may exhibit a variety of leadership styles that can have an effect on the efficiency of military operations. These styles can have an effect on the effectiveness of military operations. Studying the various approaches to leadership and methods that can be successful in reaching one's goals is essential, as is recognizing the significance of strong leadership in the accomplishment of one's military aims. It is possible that the efficiency of military operations can be improved, and that greater success can be attained on the battlefield, through the study and recognition of effective leadership.

# Chapter 24: A War on Two Fronts: The Struggle for Equality

Historically, war has frequently been a driving force behind social transformation, with previously disparate communities and groups banding together to fight for their rights and demand equality. The fight for equality has been going on for a very long time, and it has evolved into many different forms over the course of history.

The fight for equality in the United States during World War II is an example of the kind of struggle that can take place during times of war. African Americans served their country valiantly during World War II, but upon their return home they were met with continued racial discrimination and segregation. The Civil Rights Movement was able to successfully demand an end to segregation and racial discrimination by employing nonviolent protests and acts of civil disobedience, which ultimately resulted in significant changes to both the law and society.

One more illustration of this is the fight for equal rights for women during the Second World War. The war effort was greatly aided by women, who demonstrated their abilities by performing roles that were traditionally reserved for men and taking on those roles. This ultimately resulted in significant changes to both the laws and social attitudes that pertain to women's rights. It also led to an increase in the number of demands for gender equality.

There are countless other struggles for equality that have taken place during times of war, such as the fight for the rights of LGBTQ+ people, disabled people, and religious people. In addition to these examples, there are countless other struggles for equality that have taken place during times of war.

It is essential to acknowledge the influence that war has had on the progression of social change and to keep fighting for equality and justice for all. Participating in political activism, lending one's support to groups and causes that advocate for equality, and having an open and honest conversation with other people are all examples of activities that could fall under this category. All of these activities aim to foster a greater capacity for understanding and empathy for the experiences and perspectives of others.

To summarize, throughout history, war has frequently been a driving force behind social transformation and the fight for equality. During times of conflict, individuals from numerous communities and organizations have banded together to advocate for their rights and seek justice. It is essential to acknowledge the impact that war has had on societal transformation and to maintain the fight for equality and justice for all people. This fight can be continued through activism, support for organizations and causes, and engagement in dialogue to foster greater understanding and empathy. It is possible to achieve greater social justice and a more equitable world by recognizing and addressing the social impact of war. This can be done in order to make the world more fair.

# Chapter 25: The End of an Era: The Legacy of War

The legacy of war can be felt for many generations to come and leaves an indelible mark not only on societies but also on individuals. The conclusion of a war heralds the beginning of a new era, during which societies work to recover from the trauma and devastation caused by the war and to move on to better things.

The effects of World War II on Europe are a good illustration of the legacy left behind by war. The war resulted in the destruction of a continent, which resulted in the displacement of millions of people, the destruction of cities, and the collapse of economies. However, the end of the war also marked the beginning of a new era of reconstruction and reconciliation. After the war, the nations of Europe worked together to rebuild their economies and societies, as well as to forge a new path towards peace and prosperity. This new era began when the war came to an end.

One more illustration of this is the legacy of the Vietnam War, which had a significant influence on the culture and society of the United States. The war was deeply divisive and divisive, and it was the cause of widespread protests and social upheaval. The conclusion of the war heralded the beginning of a new era, one that was marked by introspection and the pursuit of healing, as the people of the United States attempted to come to terms with the trauma and social division that the war had caused.

There are countless other legacies of war that have influenced the direction that history has taken, in addition to the examples given above. In the aftermath of a conflict, it is critical to both acknowledge the impact that war has had on societies and individuals, as well as make efforts toward healing and reconciliation.

It is important for societies to engage in open and honest dialogue, to acknowledge the trauma and suffering caused by war, and to work towards finding common ground and solutions that can promote healing and reconciliation in order to address the legacy of war. This is one of the most important steps that needs to be taken in order to address the legacy of war. This may include participating in efforts to rebuild and reconstruct areas that have been devastated by war, providing support and resources to individuals and communities that have been impacted by war, and working toward a world that is more peaceful and equitable.

To summarize, the conclusion of a war heralds the beginning of a new era, and the legacy of the conflict will continue to be felt for many years to come. In the aftermath of a conflict, it is critical to both acknowledge the impact that war has had on societies and individuals, as well as make efforts toward healing and reconciliation. It is possible that it will be possible to address the legacy of war and create a brighter future for everyone if we engage in dialogue that is open and honest and work towards making the world a more peaceful and equitable place.

# Chapter 26: Heroes Among Us: Honoring Our Frontline Veterans

Veterans who served in the front lines are true heroes because they put their lives on the line to serve their country, safeguard their communities, and defend the ideals that we hold most dear. It is not only appropriate, but also necessary, to recognize and honor the sacrifices and contributions made by these individuals on holidays such as Memorial Day and Veterans Day, but also on a daily basis.

It is possible to show respect for veterans who served on the front lines by ensuring that they have access to medical care, mental health services, and other resources that can assist them in overcoming the effects of war on their bodies, minds, and emotions. This may involve increasing the resources available to veterans' organizations and providing additional support for those organizations, as well as working to reduce the stigma associated with mental health issues.

One more method of paying tribute to front-line veterans is to recognize the contributions and accomplishments they have made, as well as to give them the opportunity to tell others about their experiences and the lessons they have learned. This may involve hosting events and gatherings in which veterans can come together and share their experiences with one another, or it may involve creating spaces in which veterans can contribute to the communities in which they live and to society as a whole.

In addition to this, it is essential to acknowledge the wide variety of experiences and points of view held by frontline veterans and to work toward the establishment of an environment that is welcoming and encouraging, and which values and respects each and every member of the veteran community. This may involve making an effort to address issues within the military and veteran communities such as racism, sexism, and discrimination, and to promote greater diversity and inclusivity in all aspects of society.

In conclusion, veterans of the front lines are true heroes because they have rendered significant service to their communities as well as their country and have given up a great deal as a result. It is essential to pay respect to and acknowledge their contributions, as well as to provide them with the resources, support, and opportunities they require to thrive. We can make the future better for everyone if we recognize and appreciate the contributions made by veterans who served in the front lines of combat and if we work toward making our society more accepting and supportive of one another.

# Also by Jim Stephens

Kindle Publishing Made Easy: Autopilot Cash With Amazon Kindle!
Million-Dollar Secrets of the Amazon Associates: How They Make Money From the Biggest Online Shopping Mall
Self-Publishing Made Easy: The Easy Way to Self-publish Your Own Books!
Scam Busters: How to Avoid the Most Popular Scams of Today!
Affiliate Marketing and Blogging
The Quick and Easy Guide of Diamonds
Government Information
Hiking and Camping
Koi Pond
Law Information Guide
Motor Homes Research
Affiliate Marketing and Success Systems
Online Shopping
Outsourcing Ebooks and Software Jobs
Personal Loans
Private Jet Charters
Private Yacht Charters
Internet Marketer Alpha Dog
Networking and Social Dominance in the Twenty-First Century
Copywriting Best Kept Secrets: A Training Course for Writing Great Copy
Starting Your Home Business

Affiliate Marketing for Beginners: You Will Never Succeed Unless You Take The Opportunity

A Guide to Creating the Most Appropriate Budgets for You: Additional Cash in Your Pocket

Various Advantages of Membership Websites: With Membership Websites, Create a Passive Income

Affiliate Marketing Made Simple: Avoid Common Errors and Thrive in Successes

Article Marketing Made Simple: It Is Not Necessarily Difficult to Succeed

Blogging Made Simple: Blogging Can Be Lucrative

Advertising That Pays: Increase Your Traffic and Leads

The Complete Guide to Copywriting: Creating Words That Sell

Affiliate Marketing Made Simple

The Affiliate Marketer's Manual

Aquarium Maintenance Made Simple

Beginner's Guide to Online Video Marketing

Blogging Fundamentals: Blogging is the Next Big Thing

Techniques for Advanced Search Engine Optimization: On Autopilot, Increase Your Traffic and Profits!

Article Marketing Secrets

Beginner's Guide to Black Hat SEO

Super Guide to Snowmobiling: The Best Places to Have a Great Time

Forest Adventure With Friends: A Captivating Story With a Lot of Fun

How to Advertise Like a Pro

My Journey Through Life: A Personal Memoir

The Art of Crafting Short Stories: A Guide to Writing and Publishing

The Ultimate Guide to Making Money Online: Proven Strategies and Tips for Success

Battlefield of Honor: Bravery and Sacrifice Tested In Ultimate Battle

Echoes of the Past: Unveiling History's Secrets

Warrior's Code: The Unbreakable Ethics of a Warrior

AI-Powered Marketing: The Future of Digital Advertising

Beyond Words: How ChatGPT is Revolutionizing Communication
The Language of AI: Exploring the Power of ChatGPT
Talking to Machines: The Fascinating Story of ChatGPT and AI Language Models
Uncovering the Unknown: Tales of Mysterious Discoveries
Shadow Squadron: Inside Covert Operations
The Last Stand: The Triumph of Bravery in Desperate Times
Valor in the Skies: Courage and Sacrifice in Aerial Warfare
Courage, Sacrifice, and Honor: Tales from the Frontline Heroes

## About the Publisher

Accepting manuscripts in the most categories. We love to help people get their words available to the world.

Revival Waves of Glory focus is to provide more options to be published. We do traditional paperbacks, hardcovers, audio books and ebooks all over the world. A traditional royalty-based publisher that offers self-publishing options, Revival Waves provides a very author friendly and transparent publishing process, with President Bill Vincent involved in the full process of your book. Send us your manuscript and we will contact you as soon as possible.

Contact: Bill Vincent at rwgpublishing@yahoo.com

www.ingramcontent.com/pod-product-compliance
Lightning Source LLC
LaVergne TN
LVHW042000060526
838200LV00041B/1802